During a stormy night on the African grasslands, a boy lion cub was born to a loving mother and a strong, powerful father. The grasslands were their home, and they stretched farther than the eye could see. In the mornings, the skies were clear and bright. And in

the evenings, the rains came to wet the earth. The land had everything
the lions needed to survive: food to sustain them and high grass for shelter.
The family never ventured beyond its borders, where the two-footed
creatures lived—after all, they could be dangerous.

The cub's mother licked him clean every day, never missing a speck of dirt.

When it was cold, the cub's father would cover him with his thick golden mane.

These three were a family.

Late one night, a flash of lightning signaled the coming of a horrific storm. The family found shelter in the hollow of a huge old tree. The inside was warm and dry, but the father lay outside in the rain to protect them from intruders. Streaks of lightning lit up the sky. Terrified, the cub buried his body deep under his mother's tummy.

Then, in one of the flashes, the cub saw a big brute of a lion coming out of the darkness. Its face was scarred and its mane was ragged from many battles.

The intruder pounced on the cub's father. Both lions ripped and slashed. The lioness launched herself right into the middle of the fray, but she was no match for the attacker.

Within minutes, the cub's parents were dead.

He was all alone.

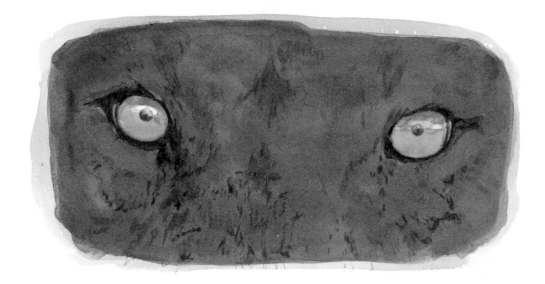

The scarred lion roared his victory—then turned his fierce eyes on the cub. The little cub snarled; his ears lay back. Yet his little body shivered in fear. He knew he stood no chance against the lion.

He bolted through a small opening in the back of the tree.

With the lion close behind, the cub ran as fast as he could into the dark, stumbling, falling, hitting rocks, banging into tree stumps and thorn patches, until there was nothing below his paws and he was falling, falling! And then rolling down, down, across rocks . . . until he came to an abrupt stop.

Everything went black.

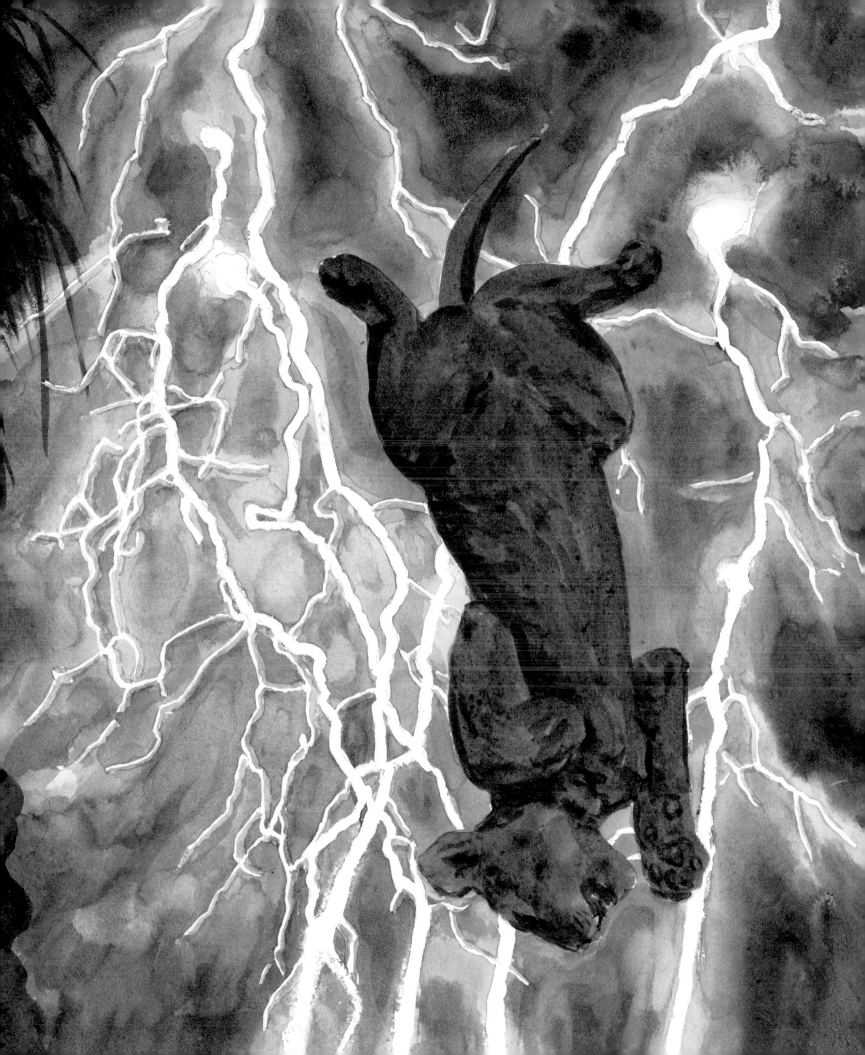

When the cub awoke, bruised and bleeding, the blistering-hot sun hung in the sky. A dozen hungry vultures circled above. He had seen them before—always around dead things.

They landed on the ground near him, their small, curious heads turning sideways to see if he was still alive. The cub felt panic. He knew he had to get away from the birds to survive.

Slowly he staggered down a small trail.

Farther down the path, a hyena was searching the area, nose high in the air. The cub spotted the animal and held very still, his heart pounding. He was lucky. The recent rain had masked his scent from the hyena.

The cub staggered on until he found . . . water! He drank and drank and for hours lay in the stream, letting its coolness heal him.

All that night, he slept. When morning came, hunger overtook his senses. Frogs, lizards, and bugs were difficult to catch; he was so weak and sore. He dragged himself from the water and down a path that ran alongside the river, until he finally collapsed in a soggy heap.

He missed the comfort and safety of his mother.

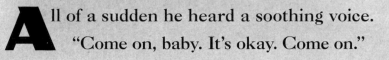

All of a sudden he heard a soothing voice.

"Come on, baby. It's okay. Come on."

On the shore ahead of him was a figure sitting on the ground.

"Come on, little guy. Don't be afraid."

"Yeaow," he cried, and hesitantly stumbled forward. He felt himself being picked up, and soon he was wrapped in something warm.

Later, he awoke nestled in a woman's arms. "Well, little guy, you're looking better!" He should have been afraid, but he wasn't. The woman was warm and gentle, just like his mother. She fed him milk and meat.

In the weeks that followed, the cub's life changed dramatically.
He was now living in a safari camp with Brini, his rescuer, and her
husband, Jack, near a village in Zambia.

Everything was new and different from anything he had ever known.
But soon he began to feel at home.

During the day, Brini let him roam free. He explored every nook
and cranny of the camp, scampering to catch bugs and chase the dog.
There were even children for him to play with. He loved to be in the middle
of them, playing ball, wading in a nearby stream, or sharing lunch under
the giant Mugumo tree on the shore of the Zambezi River.

Brini and Jack soon decided that the cub needed a name.
They thought hard, trying to come up with a proper name for a lion.
"I know!" said Brini. "We'll call you Zamba. You were born in Zambia,
and I found you on the Zambezi River. Zamba is perfect!"

She picked up the lion cub and held him close. "I now crown
you Zamba! The world's greatest lion!"

As he grew, Zamba no longer resembled the cuddly kitten he once was.
He was becoming a wild lion and much more than they could handle.
Although he didn't mean to, he was sometimes too rough with the children.
Letting Zamba live in the camp just wasn't safe anymore, but he couldn't
return to the wild. Having had no parents to teach him, he'd never learned
how to live on his own. Brini had to do something. But what?

She remembered meeting a man from California named Ralph.
He ran a ranch called Africa U.S.A., where he gave animals a safe, loving
home and also trained them to be less aggressive. Often these tame animals
would star in movies, TV shows, and commercials. Ralph had
once told Brini that his lifelong dream was to take in a lion. Africa U.S.A.
seemed like the perfect place for Zamba to learn how to live with other
animals and humans. She called Ralph right away.

"Yes, yes, of course! I would love to have your lion!"

On the day Brini, Jack and Zamba left Africa, the local tribes turned out to say their good-byes. Zamba was put in a special cage, and the three of them boarded the plane. The cage was kept in the cargo hold under the plane. Zamba didn't know quite what to make of the small, cramped space or the strange noises. The roar and motion of the plane, and later the truck that took him to the ranch, scared him.

Finally Zamba arrived at the ranch, and all the loud noises and movement stopped.

It was hard for Brini and Jack to say good-bye to their friend, but they knew they were doing the right thing for him.

After they left, Zamba began sniffing the air. He smelled green grass, lush trees, and a man. A man he'd never seen before.

"Come on, Zamba. Come on out." He heard a voice. Zamba peeked his head out of the cage and found that he was on a hill, encircled by branches.

"I'm Ralph. Come on, now. Let's see you." Zamba stepped out of
the cage. "And this is Old Lady," the man said, pointing to the three-
hundred-year-old oak tree that overlooked the ranch. "Old Lady is a
special tree. All my animals and the people who work here find it to
be very peaceful. I hope it has the same effect on you."

Ralph opened his arms wide, and for the first couple of hours the
two rolled and played. "Welcome to your new life, my friend."

Now it was time for the training to begin.

First, Zamba met the other animals. Of all of them, Prince, a movie stunt dog, would become his closest companion—and his teacher.

If Zamba got tough, Prince would put him in his place just like a mother lion, with a growl and a soft paw.

Zamba would follow Prince's lead as they accompanied Ralph on his rounds, attending to all the animals. He saw that Ralph fed each of them the same way—by hand. This taught Zamba that only good things came from that hand. Never pain.

And just like a child, he had to learn that he couldn't take other animals' toys and food or destroy things. He had to learn to follow instructions— come when called and stop when he heard "No!" It took a lot of practice, but Zamba was a star student.

Every day, as they trained, the three friends grew closer and Zamba became gentler and less aggressive.

At night Zamba lay at the foot of Ralph's bed, and on special occasions
he was allowed to sleep on the bed, which had been specially built to hold
his weight. On Saturdays the ranch kids would stay over with Ralph's
daughter, Tana, and snuggle up to Zamba to keep warm while
they watched TV. If a cartoon featured a dog barking, Zamba would get up
and look around the room to see if Prince was there.
The children would roll on the floor laughing!
As Zamba grew settled and comfortable, he became
a real people lion. He liked to play with them, eat with
them—and work with them.
His friendliness made him
perfect for the movies.

Zamba's gentle nature was rare among lions, and he was able to work with people in different situations, which the movie people loved. He went to auditions and performed what the movie script called for, usually a snarl, an attack, or a walk through the jungle.

He even had his own dressing room where he was brushed and groomed for each scene. One time, the script for a hair commercial called for his mane to be in curlers. Zamba hated them, but Ralph couldn't stop laughing!

When word got out that Zamba could perform safely with children, his movie career took off. He won many awards and shared the screen with some of Hollywood's most famous actors. His most famous role was as MGM Studios' "Leo the Lion." Zamba had officially become a star.

One of his film shoots took him all the way back to Africa, not far from where he was born. During a break from filming, Ralph led Zamba on a walk through the high grass. Even off his leash and with animals in sight, Zamba stayed at Ralph's side. His training was paying off.

These were good times, but a bad time was on its way. A time that would test even Zamba.

All month there had been constant storms. The staff at Ralph's ranch worked overtime keeping the rain from the animals' quarters, providing warm blankets for the primates and straw for the elephants. Ralph kept Zamba with him in his bedroom, having learned that Zamba was afraid of lightning and thunder.

One night, a huge storm hit. The rain came in buckets and tons of earth oozed down into the ranch.

Just then, the phone rang. It was the weatherman.

"Get out NOW! The dam broke. There's a huge wave of water headed right for you!"

The animals!

Ralph—followed by Zamba—raced to the workers' houses.
"Open up all the cage doors and pens. If the animals are locked in,
they'll drown."

"Are you crazy?" someone shouted. "They'll kill each other!
Some aren't even trained yet."

"Just do it," Ralph yelled back. "It's their only hope."

Trainers opened doors as fast as they could.

The animals ran for their lives.

In the near distance, over the deafening noise of the storm,
Ralph could hear the roar of the coming water. People scattered in all
directions. It was a horrifying sight. Zamba may have been scared and
soaked to the bone, but he stayed at Ralph's side, just as he had when
they'd walked through the fields in Africa.

All of a sudden, a flood of rushing water exploded into the compound.
Full-grown trees and wrecked buildings were carried away. Cages were

smashed and animals were swept away in the deluge. Ralph grabbed
Zamba's mane just as the water engulfed them. Fearful that his wet mane
might drag Zamba under, Ralph pulled his fur to keep Zamba's head above
water. But he could hold on for only so long, and when Ralph finally lost
his grip, Zamba was swallowed by the water.

But Zamba didn't drown. When he finally emerged from the rushing water, he looked around at his surroundings, taking in the destruction. Cages were smashed. Animals were scattered. Some injured. Some dead. Zamba began to look for a safe place to rest, but there was none. Everything had been destroyed.

Everything except Old Lady! It was a long walk to the mountaintop, but that's where Zamba headed. On his way, he passed all the animals he had helped Ralph and Prince care for. They were now trembling from fear and the cold water. What would happen to them now? How would they survive?

One by one, each animal rose and followed Zamba, knowing that wherever he went, they would be safe. Camels, ostriches, hyenas, llamas. Animals of every kind. Animals that in nature would have been predator and prey now walked side by side, all finding shelter under Old Lady. Wet and exhausted, they all stopped at the top of the hill and sat under that ancient oak tree.

Hours passed. The rain slowly began to subside, and the floodwaters
began to recede. The storm clouds gave way to the morning sun, and a
rainbow appeared in the sky. Zamba sat peacefully among the animals
that had followed him to safety.

When Zamba saw Ralph coming up the hill, he stood, happy to see that his friend was safe.

"Oh, Zamba, I thought you were dead," Ralph cried, relieved that the lion had survived the flood.

"Come, now, it's time to go home," Ralph whispered in Zamba's ear.

The animals calmly followed Ralph and Zamba back
down the ridge.

As the group entered the ranch, people came from everywhere,
some in tears, some hugging their favorite animals—a mixture
of sadness, relief, and joy. When the last tears were shed,
Ralph knelt beside Zamba.

"You saved them," Ralph whispered as he wrapped
his arms around Zamba's neck. "When Brini brought you
to me, she said you were destined to be
the world's greatest lion. Oh, how
right she was."

To Suzzi and Taka.
—R.H.

In memory of my brother
Donn,
and his lion, Sheba.
—T.L.

Philomel Books

A division of Penguin Young Readers Group.
Published by The Penguin Group. Penguin Group (USA) Inc., 375 Hudson Street, New York, NY 10014, U.S.A.
Penguin Group (Canada), 90 Eglinton Avenue East, Suite 700, Toronto, Ontario M4P 2Y3,
Canada (a division of Pearson Penguin Canada Inc.). Penguin Books Ltd, 80 Strand, London WC2R 0RL, England.
Penguin Ireland, 25 St. Stephen's Green, Dublin 2, Ireland (a division of Penguin Books Ltd).
Penguin Group (Australia), 250 Camberwell Road, Camberwell, Victoria 3124, Australia (a division of Pearson
Australia Group Pty Ltd). Penguin Books India Pvt Ltd, 11 Community Centre, Panchsheel Park,
New Delhi - 110 017, India. Penguin Group (NZ),67 Apollo Drive, Rosedale, Auckland 0632, New Zealand
(a division of Pearson New Zealand Ltd). Penguin Books (South Africa) (Pty) Ltd, 24 Sturdee Avenue,
Rosebank, Johannesburg 2196, South Africa. Penguin Books Ltd, Registered Offices:
80 Strand, London WC2R 0RL, England.

Edited by Kiffin Steurer. Design by Amy Wu. Text set in 14-point Caslon 3.
The illustrations in this book are rendered in watercolor on a raw umber ground.

Library of Congress Cataloging-in-Publication Data
Helfer, Ralph.   The world's greatest lion / Ralph Helfer; illustrated by Ted Lewin.   p. cm.   1. Zamba (Lion)—
Juvenile literature. 2. Lion—California—Los Angeles—Biography—Juvenile literature. 3. Animals in motion pictures—
California—Los Angeles—Biography—Juvenile literature. 4. Helfer, Ralph—Juvenile literature.
5. Animal trainers—California—Los Angeles—Biography—Juvenile literature.   I. Lewin, Ted.
II. Title.   SF408.6.L54H44 2012   599.75709794 94—dc23   2011020681

ISBN 978-0-399-25417-8
1   3   5   7   9   10   8   6   4   2